Ocean Adventures

The Atlantic Ocean

Written by
Rebecca Phillips-Bartlett

KidHaven Publishing

Published in 2026 by
KidHaven Publishing, an Imprint of Greenhaven Publishing, LLC
2544 Clinton St., Buffalo, NY 14224

Written by: Rebecca Phillips-Bartlett
Edited by: Noah Leatherland
Designed by: Ker Ker Lee

All facts, statistics, web addresses, and URLs in this book were verified as valid and accurate at time of writing. No responsibility for any changes to external websites or references can be accepted by either the author or publisher.

Cataloging-in-Publication Data

Names: Phillips-Bartlett, Rebecca, 1999-.
Title: The Atlantic Ocean / Rebecca Phillips-Bartlett.
Description: Buffalo, NY : KidHaven Publishing, 2026. | Series: Ocean adventures | Includes glossary and index.
Identifiers: ISBN 9781534552005 (pbk.) | ISBN 9781534552012 (library bound) | ISBN 9781534552029 (ebook)
Subjects: LCSH: Atlantic Ocean--Juvenile literature. | Marine ecology--Atlantic Ocean--Juvenile literature.
Classification: LCC GC481.P45 2026 | DDC 910.9163--dc23

Printed in China

CPSIA compliance information: Batch #QW26KH: For further information contact Greenhaven Publishing LLC at 1-844-317-7404.

Please visit our website, www.greenhavenpublishing.com. For a free color catalog of all our high-quality books, call toll free 1-844-317-7404 or fax 1-844-317-7405.

Find us on

Photo Credits – Images courtesy of Shutterstock.com, unless otherwise stated.

Cover & Recurring – SNEHIT PHOTO, Nastya Vaulina, alazur. 2–3 – Dieter Kuhn. 4–5 – Kingppin, silvae. 6–7 – Adwo, Alvaro Ardisanal, Viacheslav Lopatin. 8–9 – Glenmore, BogDarena, Allen McDavid Stoddard. 10–11 – ggw, WindVector. 12–13 – Caminhos me Levem, CherylRamalho, BEST-BACKGROUNDS. 14–15 – Jesus Cobaleda, RLS Photo. 16–17 – Karl Weller, lego 19861111. 18–19 – Serenity Images23, Nikky de Graaf, Angela N Perryman. 20–21 – Kehinde Temitope Odutayo, PeopleImages.com - Yuri A. 22–23 – Ethan Daniels, Wirestock Creators.

CONTENTS

PAGE 4 Ocean Adventures

PAGE 6 The Atlantic Ocean

PAGE 8 Areas of the Atlantic Ocean

PAGE 12 Weather

PAGE 14 Fish

PAGE 16 Mammals

PAGE 18 Birds

PAGE 20 Our Changing Oceans

PAGE 22 Exploring the Ocean

PAGE 24 Glossary and Index

WORDS THAT LOOK LIKE THIS CAN BE FOUND IN THE GLOSSARY ON PAGE 24.

OCEAN ADVENTURES

Oceans are full of amazing animals, useful materials, and fascinating historical objects. They are also very important for keeping our planet healthy. Around half of the oxygen that we breathe is made in the ocean!

Are you ready to go on an ocean adventure? Then let's set sail! Oceans are large pools of salt water. Earth has five main oceans.

TODAY, WE ARE EXPLORING THE ATLANTIC OCEAN.

THE ATLANTIC OCEAN

The Atlantic is the second largest ocean on Earth. It is often split into the North Atlantic and South Atlantic. The Atlantic Ocean is in between the Americas, Europe, and Africa.

People have been exploring the Atlantic Ocean since ancient times. Throughout history, this ocean has been used to transport goods, such as rice and fabric, between Europe and North America.

THE ATLANTIC OCEAN IS NAMED AFTER A GREEK GOD CALLED ATLAS.

AREAS OF THE ATLANTIC OCEAN

The Mid-Atlantic Ridge

Did you know there are mountains under the ocean? The Mid-Atlantic Ridge is a long chain of mountains under the Atlantic Ocean. Lots of volcanoes and earthquakes happen near the Mid-Atlantic Ridge.

In Iceland, the Mid-Atlantic mountains rise above sea level.

The Sargasso Sea

Some smaller areas of ocean are called seas. The Atlantic Ocean is home to the Sargasso Sea. The Sargasso Sea is named after a seaweed, called sargassum, that floats on the water.

LOTS OF ANIMALS RELY ON SARGASSUM FOR FOOD AND SHELTER.

Iceberg Alley

Seaweed is not the only thing floating in the Atlantic Ocean. Many icebergs float through an area called Iceberg Alley. These huge blocks of floating ice can be very dangerous for ships.

In 1912, a ship called *Titanic* sank after hitting an iceberg in the Atlantic.

The Bermuda Triangle

The Bermuda Triangle is an area of the Atlantic Ocean between Bermuda, Florida, and Puerto Rico. It is famous for having many stories about ships and planes disappearing there in the past. However, many people safely cross the Bermuda Triangle every day.

WEATHER

Different parts of the ocean are different temperatures. The Atlantic Ocean is split by an invisible line called the equator. The warmest part of the Atlantic is just north of the equator.

WARM PART OF THE ATLANTIC

COLD PART OF THE ATLANTIC

Many powerful, swirling storms called hurricanes form over the Atlantic Ocean. These hurricanes are caused by strong, warm winds from the Sahara in Africa. Hurricanes can cause lots of damage if they reach land.

FISH

Reef Fish

Some warm parts of the Atlantic Ocean are home to coral reefs. Coral reefs are underwater habitats made of lots of tiny creatures called corals. Thousands of fish, including queen angelfish, live in coral reefs.

American Eels

American eels start their lives in rivers and streams. Once they are old enough to have young, they swim out to the Sargasso Sea. Female American eels can lay millions of eggs at once.

AMERICAN EELS CAN GROW TO AROUND 5 FEET (1.5 M) LONG.

MAMMALS

Gray Seals

Gray seals live in the North Atlantic Ocean. These mammals spend lots of time in the water hunting for food. They can hold their breath for over an hour before coming to the surface to breathe.

North Atlantic Right Whales

North Atlantic right whales are one of the most endangered types of whales. They eat using filter feeding. They swim through the water with their mouths open, scooping up small animals as they move.

BIRDS

Atlantic Puffins

Atlantic puffins are famous for their brightly colored beaks. During winter, puffins live out at sea. They hunt by diving underwater to catch fish. During spring, puffins nest on rocky cliffs by the sea.

PUFFINS' BEAKS ARE ONLY BRIGHTLY COLORED DURING NESTING SEASON.

Brown Pelicans

Brown pelicans mostly live on beaches and islands in the Atlantic Ocean. They catch fish by diving underwater. They scoop fish and water up in their bills. The water pours out, and they swallow the fish.

OUR CHANGING OCEANS

Large ships use the Atlantic Ocean to carry heavy items long distances. Ships create lots of noise and can be dangerous for animals. Sometimes, garbage and oil spill out of ships and into the ocean.

Adding noise, garbage, and oil to the ocean is a harmful change. We should all try to stop the ocean from changing too much. You can help by buying fewer things, reusing things, and recycling properly.

USING A REUSABLE BOTTLE IS ONE WAY OF HELPING THE OCEANS.

EXPLORING THE OCEAN

Exploring the oceans is a great way to learn more about our world. If we dive down deep enough, we could discover amazing new animals or interesting objects from throughout history.

We need to be careful as we explore! The ocean is powerful and mysterious. Lots of dangerous storms start at sea. Oceans are also home to thousands of animals who deserve our respect.

GLOSSARY

ancient	belonging to the very distant past
endangered	when there are very few of a certain type of animal left in the world
habitats	the natural homes in which animals, plants, and other living things live
mammals	animals that are warm-blooded, have a backbone, and make milk to feed their young
oxygen	the natural gas that many living things need to survive
recycling	using again to make something new
sea level	the level of the sea's surface

INDEX

ancient Egyptians 7
beaches 19
beaks 18
bills 19
fish 14, 18–19
icebergs 10
mountains 8
seaweed 9–10
ships 10–11, 20
storms 13, 23